Two Plays

The Snow Queen

November Door

Also by David Pratt

Bob the Book (novel)
My Movie (stories)
Looking After Joey (novel)
Wallaçonia (novel)
Todd Sweeney: The Fiend of Fleet High (a thriller)

Two Plays

David Pratt

The Snow Queen

November Door

hosta press

ann arbor

Printed in the United States of America

ISBN: 978-1-7329414-2-7 (paper); 978-1-7329414-3-4 (ebook)

Library of Congress Control Number: 2019952948

Cover design: Nicholas Williams

Cover illustration, detail from *John Roberts' Farm*, woodcut by Margot G. Torrey; Copyright © 2020 Estate of Margot G. Torrey; used with the permission of Neige Torrey Christenson

Interior design: Kelly Smith

Two Plays

The Snow Queen, based on the author's short story of that name, premiered June 22, 2003, at HERE Arts Center, New York City, as part of *Writers on the Ledge*, a series curated by Regie Cabico for FUSE: The NYC Celebration of Queer Culture, a co-production of HERE and Dixon Place. *November Door* premiered July 19, 2004, at Dixon Place, New York City, as part of its 2004 HOT! NYC Celebration of Queer Culture.

For both productions, Jane Lincoln Taylor played the role of Jo Osbourne, and the author played the roles of Narrator/Steven Underwood.

§

Jo is thirty-eight in *The Snow Queen* and sixty-five in *November Door*. Steven is eleven in *The Snow Queen,* but should be played by an adult. He is thirty-eight in *November Door*.

Productions of either play may be open to casting trans or nonbinary performers. The author is also open to the addition of actors to *The Snow Queen* (to play parents, etc.). Their speeches should be directed out, to imagined versions of others (see description on page 3 of how Jo and Steven inter-act). Their appearances should be discreet, never intruding on the play's meditative quality.

—DP

The Snow Queen

for Jane Lincoln Taylor

The play takes place in the NARRATOR's memory of his north-central Connecticut hometown in 1968.

Each of the actors inhabits a personal world, speaking to imagined versions of the other, even when stage directions say a line is delivered, for example, "To JO." Others' dialogue is in quotation marks when the NARRATOR reports exchanges involving unseen characters. Only where there might be confusion do stage directions specify to whom the actors are speaking or in whose voice the NARRATOR is speaking.

Lights up to half.

A threadbare Oriental rug. The NARRATOR enters, sets out two chairs, then stands by the stage left chair. Lights fade to black, then slowly up to full. JO is by the stage right chair.

NARRATOR [*to audience*]: Jo Osbourne had big shoulders and short black hair in bangs. Her father, Dr. Osbourne, had delivered me, but he was dead by the time all this happened.

My parents introduced me to Jo one late-winter Sunday in 1968, up in the church choir loft, after the service. She shook my hand. She raised an eyebrow, nodded once, and smiled like we'd been friends a long time.

JO: Pleased to meet you, sir. Care to give me a hand putting back some hymnals?

3

NARRATOR: Sure! Right away we started inventing these jokes, like pretending we were stevedores loading a ship.

The NARRATOR sends hymnals to JO with exaggerated hoisting and swinging motions, and she continues those motions and racks the hymnals.

BOTH [*boisterously, not in unison*]: Hey! Hup! Ho! Hey! Hup! Ho! Hey! Hup! Ho!

NARRATOR: Afterwards, I was leaving with my parents. I tried to get over next to Mom, so my dad and my brother Russell wouldn't hear. I said, "That was a woman, right?" She shushed me. She might have looked at Dad. He was chuckling. He gave me this kind of punch on the shoulder. Called a "love tap," I guess. [*To parents:*] "What?"

"People might hear you!" Mom said. She gave Dad a look. "We can discuss it at home." But we never did.

The next week, after Sunday school, I ran to church and up to the choir loft. Somehow, I knew it was always Jo who put away the hymnals. I was afraid I'd be late, even though it was just eleven-oh-five. I was also afraid I'd have to introduce myself again, but—

JO: Well, hey there, Sport!

NARRATOR: Hi! She acted so happy, like I was her old friend and we always did this.

JO: Come to do hymnal duty again?

NARRATOR: Yup! She hadn't even started.

JO: Wonderful! We can start over here. We'll skin

and dress a hundred of 'em and be back in port in time for supper. Did you know, in whaling days, they cut the whale blubber like pages of a book and called 'em bibles?

NARRATOR: Nope.

JO: It's true. So how's life been treating you since last Sunday? Math class still as boring as it was in 1492? I mean, 1942?

NARRATOR: She was so . . . good . . . to me. It was almost like she understood the Thing about me, how I couldn't be like other boys, no matter how hard I tried. Including my own brother, Russell. But Jo didn't mind the weird way I was. She was different, too. She did look and act kind of, y'know, like a man. But she was funny and nice, and after a while, the way she was made more sense than anyone else.

While we put the hymnals in the racks, Jo told me about her favorite hymns and her house up on Coe Hill and the meadows out back, and then we put away the extra folding chairs she had set out for the choir, and finally my dad had to come get me.

JO: Mr. U! Sorry. Guess we lost track of time. You have raised an awfully fine helper here. Would you folks mind if I offered him a few shekels to help me with some chores this afternoon, up to the Old Manse?

NARRATOR: Jo meant her house. Dad looked annoyed, not like the answer was no, but like she shouldn't have asked in the first place. He said we'd have to talk to Mom. Mom got all anxious, but I said *"Please!"*

JO: Now, Sport, if it's not convenient—

NARRATOR: Jo said she would pay me twenty-five cents an hour. Finally, Mom said it was all right, if I was home by four.

JO: Four o'clock it is, Mrs. U.

NARRATOR: Working with Jo wasn't like chores at home, but like I'd just happened along to help a friend. We had these regular jokes—

JO: Want to give me a hand here, Sport? [*The NAR-RATOR applauds.*] Oh, very amusing! [*Bows nonetheless, bent at the waist, one arm in front, the other behind.*]

NARRATOR: And so helping out on Coe Hill became a tradition. Jo loved traditions. For example, every Sunday she asked,

JO: Whatcha reading, Sport?

NARRATOR: Because I liked to read so much—stuff other than what we read in school. Another tradition was knocking off work—

JO: Halt!

NARRATOR: —and going with Jo's basset hound, Moose, in the truck, over to the cider mill in Granby—

JO: Emergency cider run!

NARRATOR: One time, she showed me how to put a new hinge on my butterfly box, and she let me keep the screwdriver.

JO: My dad gave this to me when I was about your age, and now: I give it to you.

NARRATOR: I went home and told my mom, "Jo can do anything!" Mom said, "Well, that's good, I guess." Sort of to himself, Dad said, "Well, not quite everything." He chuckled. When Dad said stuff to himself, you didn't ask him what it was or what it meant. He'd just say, "Oh, nothing."

In April, at the First Church square dance, Jo wore her one nice outfit I ever saw—gray slacks, a yellow sweater, a white turtleneck, and a tiny silver cross on a chain. She came over to me and said,

JO: Handsome sir, might one hope your dance card is not full?

NARRATOR: But Dad said, "I think Steve might like to dance with one of those pretty young ladies over there. Am I right or am I right?"

JO: Oh. Well. You go ahead, Sport. We'll see ya later.

NARRATOR: That fall, the day after Halloween, I was walking on the causeway to Wilkinson Academy, where I was going to go one day, and where Jo worked as a carpenter. She came along in her truck and slowed down next to me.

JO: What ho, Pilgrim?

NARRATOR: Oh, hi.

JO: What brings you out?

NARRATOR: I told her how, that morning [*to JO:*] You know my brother, Russell, right? He hit me with his hockey stick, so I tried to take it, y'know, yank it away from him, and the end of it, it broke this vase of my mom's. So she said I was a disgrace, and I said

7

she loved Russell more'n me, and then my dad came up and my mom was crying and saying the same thing she always does: "Why do *I* have to be the villain?" And she went into the bedroom and slammed the door. So Dad said I should apologize— [*to audience:*]—and it was awful, because Jo was really listening. [*Again to JO:*] But I snuck out to go to the hardware store, but, instead, I took a detour here, just to be by myself for a while. What are *you* up to?

JO: Hold on, now, Sport. Why don't you come around here? Hop in. [*Her eyes follow the NARRATOR around the truck; when he's in and seated next to her, she tousles his hair.*] Now, I want us to rewind the tape a second. I think you really know your mom loves you every bit as much as she loves your brother.

NARRATOR: I tensed up my muscles. It was a thing I did when I was in trouble or people lectured me. When I snuck out of the house to go to the hardware store, I'd felt like a real boy. But when Jo said that stuff about Mom loving me, I felt like a girl. Lonely, like they could get me.

I didn't tell Jo the other stuff, like how, even though he was a year younger than me, Russell was bigger and more masculine, with muscles and all hard. I was plumper and shaped funny. It would be impossible to be like him, ever. It was like Russell was totally from outside our family, and that's why Mom liked him so much.

I also didn't tell how I knew the vase would break. [*Pause.*] I knew.

JO: Maybe I should give you a lift t'home, so they'll know you're okay.

The NARRATOR deflates. JO starts the truck up again. She checks on him. She leans toward him and starts to sing.

JO [*singing*]: Whe-e-e-en I was a lad I served a term—

BOTH [*singing*]:

> —as office boy to an attorney's firm
> I cleaned the windows and I swept the floor
> And I polished up the handle of the big front door
> Yes, he polished up the handle of the big front door!

NARRATOR: When we got up in the center of town she said,

JO: Methinks I am getting an Idea!

NARRATOR: She swung into the parking lot by the A&P and Vogel's Hardware, and pulled up to the phone booth. We got out, I called my house and Jo got on.

JO: Mrs. U! Jo Osbourne here. I found young Steven; yes, ma'am, fit as a viola, as we say. He'd like to speak to you.

NARRATOR: I took the phone. Jo stood with her hand on my shoulder. I tried to shrug it away a little, but I couldn't be obvious, so finally I just apologized. It was funny—Mom was real cheerful and talked fast. Like she was trying to make the whole thing not have happened. It was over real quick, and I gave the phone back to Jo.

JO: So, Mrs. U! I'm doing some repairs on my stone wall this afternoon. You know how there's something that doesn't love a wall, and so on? Or in this case, some*one*. At any rate, do you think you could possibly lend me a foreman for a couple of hours? Yes, ma'am, indeed—by four o'clock. Now is this boy union? Oh, nothing, ma'am. Four o'clock, yes, yup, bye-bye now. [*Hangs up. To Steven:*] Tally ho, Jeeves!

NARRATOR: We worked for two hours fetching and carrying stones in the field out back of the Osbourne house on Coe Hill. Someone had toppled a section of Jo's wall. You could tell it was some guys. It just looked . . . violent. Jo?

JO: Mm?

NARRATOR: Who d'you think did this?

JO: Did *this*? Oh, it's probably just frost heaves.

NARRATOR: But you told Mom how some*one* didn't love your wall.

JO: Well, Sport, I'll tell you: it's a waste of time and energy blaming. One puts things back the way they were. Hope there isn't a next time.

NARRATOR: But I knew, and I bet Jo knew, too; she just wouldn't say. Ever. It was those guys who lived up there—Don Filbert, Jack Wessel, Jack Sheehan. They went to my Sunday school. They were worse-behaved than me, but people liked them better, and

I kept thinking I should be like them. I should be brave and, like, boyish enough to wreck stuff, too, except never anything of Jo's. I went out into the long grass to fetch a stone.

JO: Sport, I wouldn't go down there. There's poison ivy.

NARRATOR: But I had the stone already. When I turned back I saw something spray-painted on the other side of the wall. I didn't understand the word, but I knew what spray-painting meant. I gripped my rock and thought of smashing it right down on Donny Filbert's face.

JO: Something the matter, Sport?

NARRATOR: No! I came back quickly. Jo was looking away from me. She would never think a thing like that. She always forgave. That didn't seem . . . satisfying to me. Forgiving felt weak, like I'd totally be a girl or disappear completely if I forgave someone. Except . . . being so angry and feeling like I could never do anything about it—that wasn't satisfying, either. I was about to go for another rock, just one close by, when—

JO: Halt! All hands for an Emergency Cider Run!

NARRATOR: And we ran for the truck with Moose. When we got home, Jo made hot cider and we had her homemade shortbreads. They were my favorite. She finally got me home—*my* home, I mean—at four twenty-five. "Well," my mother said. "I was worried about you two!"

JO: No need, ma'am! I've kept a close eye—

NARRATOR: "It's almost five!" Mom said. And smiled.

JO: Well, I'm sorry, ma'am . . .

For a moment, JO doesn't know what to do. Finally, she turns and sits. The lights on her side of the stage go down to half.

NARRATOR: And then the snow came.

An instrumental of the Advent hymn "O Come, O Come, Emmanuel" fades in. Harp, hammered dulcimer, or acoustic guitar would be most appropriate. The NARRATOR speaks after the first two lines of the hymn have played.

It danced outside my window at night. It filled the world outside our classroom, and it felt like we were all on a spaceship together.

Hymn continues. When the chorus is over, the music fades.

The day school let out for Christmas, my dad and I had liverwurst sandwiches for lunch. Dad loved liverwurst and always offered it to me. I didn't like it, but I took it because it seemed like a grown-up thing to like.

As we sat at the kitchen table, Dad asked, "So, how's the ol' math going?" Dad taught math up at the junior high. I told him the "ol' math" was fine. If I'd told the truth, that I was getting C's like always, he would've wanted to help—like, right then. And when Dad helped me with math, I sort of got the feeling he didn't like me. Or . . . that he didn't like math.

"Well," he said, "if you ever need help, you know

where to turn. Not many kids have a live-in tutor!"
I didn't know how to tell him that made it worse.

At six o'clock we picked Russell, my brother, up at the
hockey rink. He climbed in back with Mom and stuck
the end of his stick into the front seat between me and
Dad. Mom took a piece of the black tape that was curl-
ing off and tried to stick it back on. "Mom!" Russell
snapped. "Leave it!" Mom folded her hands and stared
at the back of my father's head. "Calm down, Russ,"
Dad said. Russell hunched forward. I looked at his
hands, gripping the back of the seat. They were bigger
than mine. His nails were bigger, too, with half-
moons. It meant . . . he could do things. I couldn't.
"Dad," he said, "Coach Noga wants me to try out for
the All Stars. We're goin' to Springfield, okay?"

Dad put the car in reverse. "I'm sure it is, Russ,"
Mom said. [*As Russell:*] "For your information, I
was talking to Dad!" Mom put her hand over her
mouth and looked out the window. "That's enough,
Russ," Dad said.

We drove up Coe Hill to the McDonald's by the en-
trance to the highway. Getting out of the car, Mom
walked real slow, and her face looked like someone
was dying. Russell ran ahead with Dad and I didn't
know what to do. Inside she said, "Oh, I don't guess
I'm hungry. I'll just watch you eat." But later she
went up and got an apple pie, and came back smiling
like a little girl, and even joked with us.

The next afternoon I got to do my favorite Christmas
errand—to Vogel's Hardware store to buy presents.

I loved the brass bells on the glass when I came in. I

went straight to the old wooden bins. I reached into the one with the finishing nails and squeezed a clump of them in my hand. I always did that first at Vogel's, before anything else. I let go of the nails, shook the last few off my hand, then took my hand out and studied the marks on my palm. It didn't hurt quite enough, but I couldn't do it again. One time: that was the rule.

Then I reached into the bin with the huge twenty-penny nails, took one out, and weighed it in my hand. I always liked to see the smallest and biggest of everything. I went to the dowel rack and reached in back and pulled up the thickest dowel they had. (For some reason, little skinny dowels didn't interest me.) Mr. Vogel was on the phone:

"—so the kid says to his old man, 'Dad, I got a problem: Jimmy wants to sell me his bike for twenty bucks.' And the old man says, 'Whatsa problem?' and the kid says, 'Well, Dad, you bein' black and Mom bein' Jewish, I don't know if I should jew him down to ten or steal it!'" Then he saw me and turned his back. I put the dowel away and went off down the aisle called "Home."

Cards with knives and scissors in plastic bubbles; sometimes the card showed a woman using whatever it was and smiling. Maybe a child stood by smiling, too. If it was a boy I wondered, Why can't I be like that? If it was a girl, I wondered, Is that what I really am?

I got a kitchen timer for my mom. The picture showed a woman happy that the timer was going off. Or surprised. I got work gloves for my dad. They didn't have a picture. Presents didn't make men happy. I didn't know what to get Russell, so I didn't get him anything yet.

Mr. Vogel rang up the timer and the gloves. He was about to give me change when he stopped and scowled, but like maybe he was kidding. He leaned into my face. "That business before?" he said. "You know that was grown-ups kidding around. You wouldn't go repeating none of it." I shook my head, but I couldn't say anything.

"Atta boy! Heh-heh! Wouldn't want to hafta report you for eavesdropping!" He put his fist out. I put my hand under. [*The NARRATOR, as Vogel, darts the fist back, then slowly puts it out again. As Vogel:*] "Heh-heh! Good boy."

He dropped the change into my palm. Then he took a peppermint from under the counter. I didn't want it, but I thought if I didn't take it, he might tell my parents, I dunno, something about me. So I took it.

The bells scraped the glass again. Outside, the snow whirled, hard in one direction, then doubling back.

My mom had given me money to get milk and English muffins at the A&P. Crossing the parking lot in the snow, I couldn't help thinking about a person being "jewed down." I saw a hand gripping a black lever, and the end of the lever was hooked to the Jewish person's head. As the hand went up and down, the person squashed down till they ended up like an accordion. They bounced around making off-key noises, and people laughed. I squeezed my muscles and walked faster.

Lights up on JO's side of the stage. She stands and goes behind her chair, placing her hands on it as though it were a shopping cart.

Inside the A&P, I saw a familiar checkered jacket stretched across big, hulking shoulders. I got anxious if I saw Jo around town. I had to say hello. But who would be looking and what did they think of her? Anything? What did they think of me? If she saw me first, I hoped she'd invite me up to Coe Hill for chores, and at the same time I'd be afraid she wouldn't. Mom had told me Jo had her own life, and I should never stay too long or ask too much.

She turned and disappeared down the end of the aisle and I followed. I came up behind her as she took some bread. I said [*like Lurch on* The Addams Family:] You rang?

JO [*turning and poking at him with the bread, tweaking his nose, etc.*]: Avast, sir, and also alack! You have causèd me to fumble my loaf! Scoundrel! Poltroon! I challenge you to a drool! Think fast! [*Mimes flipping the loaf at him. The NARRATOR mimes catching it. The actors are perfectly coordinated, though they are not looking at each other.*] How are ya, Sport? Merry Xmas, ho ho ho, etcetera. You're just in time to help me find some chocolate chips.

NARRATOR: You making by-cracky bars?

JO: Nothing less!

NARRATOR: Tomorrow was the church choral concert and Christmas party in the parish house. Jo

16

always ran the kitchen for church parties, and she always made by-cracky bars—a layer of brownies, a layer of graham crackers, and cake on top with chocolate chips in it. They were tricky to make. Maybe she'd ask me to help.

JO: Heavens to Murgatroyd, you're getting big. Ah, me. So! Seen any chocolate chips lately? [*The NARRATOR is about to answer.*] Who asked ya! Let's go!

NARRATOR: I led the way, and Jo pushed the cart behind.

JO: And how's everything t'home?

NARRATOR: Fine. I didn't want to complain about Russell again. What I really wanted was to finish shopping as fast as possible and have Jo invite me to her house. Here in the store, I was afraid guys from Sunday school would see us. Tomorrow at church they'd walk around going, "Fee-fi-fo-fum, I smell Jo Osbourne!" I'd try to ignore them, like my mom said, but you couldn't. I'd say, "Cut it out!" or "What's that mean?" and sound like a doofus. And all the teachers ever said was, like, "Calm down, now, Donald!" or "Now, Jack, that's enough!"

After we went through the checkout, I lifted one of the bags, so I'd have to come at least as far as Jo's truck. But then she said—

JO: Methinks I am having another in my series of Brilliant Ideas! What are you up to this afternoon?

NARRATOR: Nothing. In the store vestibule she put down her bag by the phone booth and called my house.

JO: Mrs. Underwood? Greetings. Jo Osbourne here.

NARRATOR: I could hear Mom's voice, kind of sharp.

JO: Jo *Osbourne*, ma'am. Yes, ma'am. I'm actually down to the A&P, where I was ambushed by your son in the bread aisle. Oh no, ma'am, no trouble at all. In fact, it reminded me that I could use a little help baking for church tomorrow. I wonder if Steven might come up and help at the Old Manse?

NARRATOR: Mom went on a long time. She sounded very worried.

JO: Well— Well, um— Would, um, six o'clock be all right, Mrs. U?

NARRATOR: I knew we had to be at the rink at seven for Russell's game. I heard Mom say what she usually said: "Practically another D-Day!" Everything for Mom had to be exactly on time—or even early.

JO: Of course, ma'am. Six on the button. We'll be there. See you, then, Mrs. U. Yup. You bet. Six it is! [*Here the actor may improvise, "I understand," "I know how boys are," etc., while trying to end the conversation.*] So long, ma'am. [*JO hangs up.*]

NARRATOR: As she hung up, I saw Jo—not *roll* her eyes exactly. They just sort of . . . widened. [*Demonstrates. JO stands still.*] I thought my mom went on too much. I got embarrassed in front of other kids, but it had never occurred to me that other adults thought she was a pain.

In Sunday school they taught us to forgive. Jo forgave. But I knew there were limits to that Christian stuff, and I thought my family was outside those limits. Did Jo just feel sorry for me?

JO: I have to bring you back at six, as you may have ascertained. [*She lifts grocery bag. The NARRATOR does, too.*] Tally ho, Jeeves!

NARRATOR: Outside, snow flew around us. I thought snow kind of got people together, and it made what happened before not be so bad. We put our bags in the back of the truck and climbed in front.

JO: So, what are you reading these days, Sport?

NARRATOR: Um, well, school's out, so I started *Treasure Island.*

JO: Ah, ol' Robert Louis! Wonderful stuff! Got it for Christmas when I was about your age. Had to battle for it. I'll be interested to hear what you think.

NARRATOR: And she really was. When Jo said things like that, I imagined we were both English teachers. I lived on Coe Hill, too, in my own house without my family. We'd meet early mornings going to school, agreeing the weather was colder than usual that year and discussing books. [*To JO:*] What are you reading?

JO: William James! *The Varieties of Religious Experience.*

NARRATOR [*trying to look interested*]: I'd never heard of it. I wondered what William James would think of my family.

JO: They're making it into a movie with Raquel Welch!

NARRATOR: Up on Coe Hill we stomped snow off our boots in the vestibule. Jo's basset hound, Moose, galumphed in from the living room.

JO: Moose! *Kommen sie hier, bitte!*

NARRATOR: I could smell Jo's Christmas tree and all the good times before I was born. We walked through the living room, its carpet worn and faded, past the tree with its 1950s decorations. Moose's tags jingled. I suddenly thought Dr. Osbourne was there, though I didn't remember him. He gave birth to me. I mean, he delivered me. I wondered if he was watching, to see what kind of boy I was, and not liking it.

We scuffled down the dark back hallway, its ceiling low, and emerged into the kitchen, huge and chilly, with lots of gray winter light. Cannisters of flour and sugar and jars of dried herbs sat on the counters. Nothing ever changed at Jo's. Moose sneezed and his nails clicked the floor.

JO: Moose, *wie gehts es innen*?

NARRATOR: She hung up our coats on pegs by the back door, turned on the oven, switched the radio to the Saturday afternoon opera, and removed her coat. I was kind of hoping she wouldn't turn on the opera. Operas all sounded the same to me, like ordeals. Like liverwurst.

But she didn't make me listen to it all. Soon, we were dashing around the kitchen retrieving bowls and wooden spoons. By-cracky bars required three bowls.

JO: And now, will the congregation rise for the reading of the sacred text!

NARRATOR: She meant the old, yellowed square of newspaper with the recipe. As she took it out of her mother's *Fannie Farmer Cookbook* she sang:

JO [*chants, medieval-style*]: Gloria in excelsis e pluribus unum!

NARRATOR: I liked how she joked about church stuff. Most people who really believed that stuff didn't joke.

JO [*chanting*]: Habeas corpus non sequitur!

NARRATOR: I also liked that she made jokes, like, that I couldn't quite completely get. Like she was making me smarter.

JO [*chanting*]: Et cetera, et ceter-a-a-a-a-a!

NARRATOR: While Moose sniffed around at our feet, Jo sang cooking instructions to me like it was the opera:

JO: Vieni, Signor Stefano! First we melt-a the chocolat-a-a-a!

NARRATOR: Then she stopped.

JO [*raising a finger*]: Oh! Wait!

NARRATOR: She turned the radio up.

An opera duet. JO listens and clasps her hands to her chin, as though saying grace.

NARRATOR: I stared down at the flour and looked out the window till the song was over and she came back.

JO turns the radio down. The music fades.

JO: Always have to hear that one!

NARRATOR: I wanted there to be something grown-up and difficult like opera that I enjoyed that would make Jo feel a little left out. That would make her ask me questions and look up to me, the way I looked up to her. But all I could think of right then was . . . "jewing down."

JO [*sings, as if it's a recitativo*]: Ah! Scellerato! I see you steal the chippi di cioccolato!

NARRATOR: Would it be bad if I asked Jo what Vogel meant? Even if I didn't say who it was, would she figure out it was Vogel and tell him? What if she thought it was really my parents who said it? For some reason I felt like that was the truth, but it wasn't! I tried just to concentrate on the baking, but I was afraid the whole afternoon was getting ruined, and it was my fault.

As we spread the brownie mixture in the bottom of a big Pyrex dish, I checked the clock. The afternoon was half over, and it hadn't become what I really wanted. I was still waiting for something. Was Jo still thinking about my mother? Did she wish she didn't have to deal with my mother *or* me?

JO: Okey-doke, Sport. Now, you are going to be in charge of graham crackers. You want to take the glass and crush 'em till they're all uniform and powdery.

NARRATOR: Then we sprinkled them over the brownie layer, then spread the cake batter with chocolate chips on top, and slid the whole thing into the oven.

JO: All righty. You know what comes next!

BOTH [*together*]: Clea-ea-ean u-u-up!

JO: You'll see, Sport, no one ever wants to do clean-up. You want to make a name for yourself? Be Johnny-on-the-spot for the things no one else'll do.

NARRATOR: I felt like she was making me see some little mean part of life. She might even belong to that part sometimes. Then what would I do?

After clean-up, Jo peeked at the by-cracky bars. They were tricky to bake without burning the bottoms. When she took them out, one corner was slightly burned, but she didn't care.

JO: Something burns a little, you know it's home-made. Stuff in the supermarket has to be perfect. They throw out the burnt Keebler's. No, they make the elves eat 'em! We won't take these burnt ones to church, of course. You and I can have 'em later.

NARRATOR: We left the by-cracky bars to cool. Jo fetched two pairs of old work gloves and some pruning shears from the shelf by the back door. She took our coats off the pegs, we bundled up, and she led me out into the snow.

Fade in instrumental of the carol "Here We Come A-Wassailing." Again, harp, hammered dulcimer, or guitar would be most appropriate.

NARRATOR: In the backyard she flopped down and made a snow angel.

JO: C'mon, Sport, didn't you ever do this?

NARRATOR: No. My Mom— If my coat got wet— I mean, it *would* get wet, and she'd be—

JO: We'll hang it up by the fireplace! C'mon, kiddo!

NARRATOR: NO! [*Pause.*] I—I'm sorry . . .

JO [*getting up*]: Oh, no. It's all right. Don't have to do anything we don't want to do. Just a thing I remembered from being a kid. C'mon, let's get those boughs before sunset.

NARRATOR: We walked down along the stone wall we'd fixed back in October. I hopped on top of it and Jo held her hand up by my back.

JO: Now, Robert Frost said "something" doesn't love a wall. That's why you spend your life fixing them. Never perfect. But I wonder—what if you just *didn't* fix 'em? If you just let things go the way they wanted to go?

NARRATOR: I didn't know how to answer. The idea of letting things go upset me, so I looked away and hoped she wouldn't ask again.

Music fades.

The Osbourne property went all the way down to the railroad tracks. In Jo's woods we cut holly and pine. I got to choose the carols we sang while we worked. Steam came from our mouths and Jo's voice sounded beautiful in the woods. [*To JO:*] How about—? [*Sings, off key.*] O come, O come . . . [*As JO joins, he gets in tune.*]

BOTH:

> Emmanuel, and ransom captive Israel,
> That mourns in lonely exile here,
> Until the Son of God appear.

Rejoice! Rejoice! Emmanuel shall come to thee, O Israel!

NARRATOR: And she explained to me:

JO: Not really a Christmas carol, you know, Sport? It's for Advent. When you're waiting. That's why it's so beautiful. Wanting a thing, waiting for it. Better in a way than getting it.

NARRATOR: I don't think so!

JO: Oh, I know! You're thinking about those by-cracky bars!

NARRATOR: Yup!

JO: But think, now. Which do you like better—Christmas Eve, or Christmas Day?

NARRATOR: Christmas Eve.

JO: Why?

NARRATOR: Something big is about to happen. But you don't know what, exactly.

JO: Exactly. And sometimes, a person can live a long time, thinking something big is about to happen. Unknown. That's why you've got to "Carpe Diem," as they say. That's Latin for "Seize the fish!"

NARRATOR: I wondered if Jo was waiting. For what? A husband? Or . . . like . . . a . . . like, a wife? Was *I* supposed to marry her? Suddenly I was terribly afraid I was going to ask. [*He joins JO in pulling a bough free. He sings.*] O Come, O come . . .

BOTH:

> Thou God, Thou Three-in-One,
> And ransom captive Zion.
> Disperse the gloomy clouds of night
> And death's dark shadows put to flight.
> Rejoice! Rejoice! Emmanuel shall come to thee,
>   O Israel!

JO: I think this should about do it.

NARRATOR: That disappointed me. The afternoon might as well have been over. Jo must have seen how I looked, because suddenly she got an idea for us to devise our own version of "The Twelve Days of Christmas," with stuff we did or stuff in town we both knew about. Sometimes, what we came up with fit perfectly—

JO [*singing*]: Twelve Stevens baking!

NARRATOR: Sometimes we had to change it a little—

BOTH [*singing, adding a note*]: Five by-cracky bars!

NARRATOR: But it was fun messing it up, and funny. Trying to sing as fast as we could. There was no one to tell us different, and the whole thing ended with—

BOTH [*loudly, grandly, with flourishes*]: And Jo O-o-os-bou-ou-ourne in a pi-i-ine tree-ee-ee!

Pause.

NARRATOR: In the silence, I thought Jo, and even God, was still waiting for me to ask, well, something.

JO: What is it, Sport?

NARRATOR: In Vogel's, um, Hardware . . . they have these really thick dowels? [*He mimes pulling off a glove. He holds his thumb and index finger an inch and a half apart and studies that space between.*] I hated how small and white my hands were. [*To JO:*] Like this. They're strange, what would you use 'em for?

JO: Oh, all kinds of things! I'll show you when we get up t'home.

NARRATOR: I tensed my muscles. I looked down at my boots in the snow. For a moment I knew I belonged right there; not back cutting holly or up ahead in the kitchen. Right there.

On the back porch, we stomped snow off our boots and left the holly and pine boughs. In the kitchen the opera was still on, softly. It wasn't like an ordeal now. It was nice to come back to the thing you left. I checked the clock: four-thirty. I had to leave soon. I was starting to feel it.

JO: Now: come hither, young fellow, and I will show you a little something.

NARRATOR: She got her big old flashlight, and she led me part way down the basement stairs.

JO [*feeling her way, pulling a string for an overhead light*]: Careful. Hang on a sec. Okey-doke. Now: look up there. [*She aims the flashlight.*]

NARRATOR: Above her two white set tubs ran a long, thick dowel. Empty hangers crowded one end, with paper covers from the cleaners; they made me nervous. The other end disappeared in the shadows beneath the beams.

JO: Nothing special, but you see there are all kinds of uses for all kinds of things. Now, I think you and I have a bounden duty to go sample those by-cracky bars!

NARRATOR: Right!

JO: Make sure the Evil Lord Moosifer has not corrupted them with a phial of noxious liquors.

NARRATOR: Doth Lord Moosifer lurk in yonder shadows?

JO: He doth. But we will thlip him a thorporific in hith *Hundekuchen*.

NARRATOR: Upstairs Jo put carols on the record player. I cut the by-cracky bars. We each had a piece of the slightly burned corner with a cup of hot cider, and I made Moose sit up for a dog biscuit. Then we got what Jo called "our spoils"—the holly and pine boughs—and brought them into the living room. It was exciting to just carry them inside like that—Jo didn't worry about getting needles on the carpets.

JO [*sings*]: In the bleak midwinter, frosty wind made moan.

BOTH [*sing*]: Earth stood hard as iron, water like a stone.

NARRATOR: The pine boughs made my hands sticky and spotted brown. I examined my fingers and wished again that my nails were bigger. Tomorrow would be Sunday school. What would the guys say if they saw me weaving pine boughs on Jo's mantelpiece? But with Jo, it was normal; it was what I should be doing. Just no one else thought so. The holly was beautiful. The stone wall and the stove. My brother's hockey games, all yelling and bashing. Did my parents really *like* them?

I wouldn't be here tonight, with the pine smell all around and more cider. I wished I was Moose, sleeping on the rug in front of an open fire, with nothing to do and Jo to take care of . . . of him. I wished I was a jar of dried herbs, filled up in summer and people coming to get stuff from me all winter.

Other people liked hockey. God probably liked hockey. If my parents *didn't* like it . . . was I, like, their punishment?

Squares of pale, blue-white light moved across the wall. A car engine drew up to the house.

JO: Huh. I wonder—? Uh-oh!

NARRATOR: She dropped the holly she was working on and clumped quickly to the front door. I heard her open it, and I heard—

JO: What a pleasant surprise. I guess the time got away from us.

NARRATOR: It was after six! I knew it! My mom had had to come get me. I'd *never* be allowed to come back!

JO: Completely my fault. Took the phone off the hook so no one would call me for shoveling.

NARRATOR: My body went all weak; my heart

pounded. I didn't think I could stand. I dropped my pine branch and ran to the kitchen. Ten after! Everything had gone wrong. I ran to the sink and grabbed the big, rough bar of soap that got out pine pitch. I scrubbed like crazy but it wasn't enough. I dried my hands anyway, on a paper towel, and I went through the dining room. On the way, I saw Jo's old china cookie jar and thought I was leaving it behind and would never see it again. I tried to hold on to one last moment in the cold, dim study, and then I stepped into the front hall.

JO: Look who's here, Sport.

NARRATOR: There stood my father.

JO: Would you care to sample some freshly baked by-cracky bars?

NARRATOR: Dad said no. He told me I should get my coat.

JO: I'll get it, Sport.

NARRATOR: While she was gone, I didn't look at Dad, and he didn't speak to me. She came back with my jacket in one hand and a little, flat, narrow package, wrapped and tied with a bow.

JO: Almost forgot this. Merry Christmas!

NARRATOR: She handed me whatever it was, with its curly ribbon and tag. Kind of like a popsicle stick, only bigger.

JO: Go on, Sport. It's for you.

NARRATOR [*mimes taking the present*]: Thanks. Then my dad said, "Might you also have the groceries your mother requested?" [*Gasps.*] The English muffins! And milk! I'd completely forgotten! But I knew we couldn't have a "scene" in front of Jo. "Well," Dad said, "we certainly don't have time now. We have to get some dinner and get going to the game."

JO: Well, then. Merry Christmas to all and to all a good night! And, Mr. U., my apologies again.

NARRATOR: Dad said it was "perfectly all right." He said that whenever someone did something wrong. Someone outside the family, I mean.

We picked our way to the car over frozen slush. I could feel Dad angry at me. Or Jo. Or Mom, or . . . And I could feel Jo watching me. As we backed out of the driveway, there she was in the study window, waving to me one last time. I thought Dad wouldn't want me to wave back, but that was rude, wasn't it? I was still trying to decide when suddenly . . . it was Dr. Osbourne. Looking. Then he was gone. But it was him. He was telling Jo something. About me. She wasn't agreeing. But she couldn't say no. Then they went away.

Dad drove down Coe Hill in silence. Waiting at a light in the center of town he said, "I think this is going to be the last little session at Jo Osbourne's for a while."

Did Mom say so?

He didn't answer. Neither of us spoke the rest of the way home. Slowly and carefully, so Dad wouldn't see, I took out Jo's "popsicle stick" present and peeked at the tag.

JO: "To Steven . . ."

NARRATOR: . . . it said.

JO: "So you'll always know where you are, Love, Jo. Xmas, 1968."

NARRATOR: And I thought how the only person who really liked me was disappearing further and further behind.

The next afternoon in the Parish House, they had the church party and the choral concert. There were the by-cracky bars I helped make. Mom said I shouldn't have any, unless there was one left over at the very end.

Jo ran the kitchen, like always. She put a white apron on over her gray slacks and turtleneck, and she pushed her sleeves up to her elbows. During clean-up she was everywhere—scrubbing, drying, fitting pots into other pots and stowing them in cabinets. A few of the other ladies helped. Some just chatted and sort of stepped to the left or right when Jo said,

JO [*who has been miming all this*]: 'Scuse me, folks!

NARRATOR: She did look up once and smile at me. It was a little sad, and then she went on. I turned away. My parents were talking to some friends. I studied posters on the bulletin board of birds and flowers and sayings about love and forgiveness.

What did those ladies think of Jo? Did they know the word I'd seen in *Life* magazine—the article with the pictures of women, like, together? Guys used that word if a girl was fat or ugly. Maybe I'd used it, once or twice, just to sound, you know, real. But Jo wasn't that!

[*In a comically low voice.*] "Hey!" Someone socked me on the arm. Jack Wessel! "Saw ya at the grocery store!"

"Go away!" I said. I tried to get back toward my parents, but he blocked me.

"What? Y'gonna tell *Mister* Osbourne?" He crowded me back against the bulletin board. "Hey! Does she got a dick? I bet you know. I bet you—"

"Shut up!" I shoved him. I'd never done that before. His eyes widened and his lip curled. He darted his fist at me, middle knuckle extended. I lost my balance and fell against a coat rack. He kicked me once, twice, I pulled myself up and lunged at him, and then my dad and Jo were there, pulling us apart.

"What the hell is this about?" Dad asked, and Jo said,

JO: Oh, I'm disappointed in you, Sport!

NARRATOR: I looked away. Mrs. Davies, the Sunday school superintendent, stepped between Jo and me. "I'll take care of this," she said. "Now, Jack, that's enough." She made me and him both apologize. Then my mother told me to go to the car. As I went for the door I heard her say, "Jo, please!" A hand touched my shoulder.

JO: Sport?

NARRATOR: Everyone coming at me and no one

caring how I felt or what really happened! Even Jo didn't understand. I twisted away and shoved open the door.

"Jo," I heard Mom say, "let him alone to think about it!" I stomped to the car.

When the rest of the family came, no one spoke to me. Russell and Mom got in back, and I got in front next to Dad. We shut the doors and Dad started the engine. Finally, Mom said, "Steven, how many times have I told you—just ignore people when they try to get your goat!" A knock came on the window. "Now what?" Mom muttered.

Jo was there, in her apron, without a jacket. I rolled the window down. Snow blew off the car all rainbow-colored and got caught in her hair.

JO: Hey, Killer!

NARRATOR [*softly*]: She forgave me! [*He covers his face.*]

JO: I almost forgot this.

NARRATOR [*uncovering his face*]: She held something long like a spear, wrapped in Christmas paper. She raised it—

JO: Go on! Take it, Sport!

NARRATOR: —and brought it down through the open window. It was so long I had to stick the end into the back seat. "Goodness!" Mom said. "Hey, watch it!" said Russell. His mouth was full. He was eating a by-cracky bar.

JO: Just a little something I had lying around. Well,

Merry Christmas to all, and to all a good night!

NARRATOR: And she turned away. "Say thank you!" my mother hissed. [*Calls.*] "Thank you!" I just wished I could follow.

[*Kicking the floor.*] Russell kicked the back of the seat. "It's cold in here, in case anyone hasn't noticed!" "Calm down, now, Russ," Dad said. I rolled the window back up. [*Kicks floor. As Russell:*] "So I don't get something." "What, Russ?" Mom said. "How come she always acts like a *man*?"

[*As his mother:*] "Russell!" Dad chuckled and winked at me. I gripped my present till the paper almost tore.

Russell pushed the end of it aside and leaned over into the front seat, his breath all chocolatey. "So, Dad," he said. "Didja decide about the All-Stars?"

Christmas Eve morning I went back to Vogel's. I squeezed the finishing nails, hard, then wandered the aisles. I didn't want to get Russell anything, but you couldn't do that. Or get him a twenty-penny nail. He'd say it was stupid. He'd be right. Then I saw the flashlights. I remembered Jo with her flashlight, leading us down the cellar stairs, and I thought of the cooking smells and the carols and the woods.

JO puts on a choir robe. She holds a musical score. She assumes a stance as though in a choir, her eyes on a conductor.

Maybe Jo and I would bake and sing and cut holly again. But I could get Russell a flashlight, he'd forget about it, and then I could go down in our cellar with

it, or out at night, just in our yard, I mean, and . . .
sort of . . . be a little like Jo . . .

*JO mouths to a recording of sacred Christmas music,
something a small-town choir would perform.*

Christmas Eve, 1968, the Apollo 8 astronauts
orbited the Moon. Walter Cronkite said, if a certain
engine or something didn't fire at just the right time,
they'd be stuck up there, going around and around
forever—starving, I guess, or running out of oxygen,
while everybody watched.

Christmas morning the sun streamed in on our torn
paper and ribbon. Russell said the flashlight was
stupid because he already had one that was bigger.
Honestly, I'd had no idea . . .

We opened nonfamily presents last. When I un-
wrapped Jo's gift, we were all baffled (except Russell, who was watching cartoons). It still looked like
a popsicle stick, except about an inch wide and eight
inches long and all stained and polished. Nobody
could figure out what it was or what the tag meant:

JO: "So you'll always know where you are."

NARRATOR: I laid it on top of a sweater from my
parents, like an exhibit.

Mom stood and said we were all done. But I hadn't
opened Jo's dowel. I mean, obviously, that's what it
was—anyone could see. I didn't want them actually
looking at it, but I couldn't stand them ignoring it,
either. So I said it, and Mom said, "What?" And I
repeated it. "Oh. Well," she said. "Just hurry up."
Dad was reading a book she'd given him. Russell

turned up his cartoons. I turned away from them and pulled off the paper. I *really* didn't want to have to *explain* it. Mom said, "*Two* presents from Jo. Goodness!" Like, to herself. When the paper was all off, I was still kind of trying to hide it. Mom said, "Well, what is it?" When I showed it, she said, "Good Lord, *another* mystery! What's the tag say?"

JO *and* NARRATOR: "To Steven. So many uses."

NARRATOR: She looked at Dad. "He must have said something she misunderstood."

Dad didn't look up. He just said, "I would say Jo Osbourne 'misunderstands' a great many things!"

As his dad, the NARRATOR chortles in a self-satisfied way. As his mother says the following, we sense she is debating whether or not to say more.

"Well," Mom said, "Be that as it may . . . We'll be sure and write a thank-you note."

Music fades. JO removes her choir robe and sits.

Late in the afternoon, after dinner, I was alone in the living room having one of the milk chocolate balls that came in my stocking. Mom came in and began picking bits of paper and tape from the carpet. Dad was asleep upstairs and Russell was in his room playing with his soldiers. I heard him making explosions.

"Did you get what you wanted for Christmas?" Mom asked.

Uh-huh. [*Pause.*] Mom . . . why does everyone act funny about Jo?

"About what?"

About *Jo*. Osbourne.

"Oh. Well. I'm not aware that anyone acts *funny* about her. Your father probably thinks you should just have more friends your own age." She sat down next to me and we began sorting paper. We threw away Dad's and Russell's crumpled wads and saved the smooth sheets she and I had removed from our gifts.

But he laughed at her!

"Steven! When did your father ever *laugh at* anyone?"

Today!

"I'm sure he was hoping that *you* would laugh *with*—"

When I opened her present and you said—

"Well, it was an unusual present! There must have been some mistake. We'll have to think how to thank her." She smoothed one sheet of paper over and over on her lap.

He said she "misunderstood" things. And you just said—

"Steven, you have to learn to take a little friendly ribbing in stride; it's part of growing up. You don't have to get dramatic about it. Hand me the scissors?"

And Sunday, after the thing, in the car—

"Steven! I don't even know what it is we're discussing anymore! Let's just try and enjoy Christmas!"

She got up and turned on the radio. A choir sang:

> The cattle are lowing, the baby awakes,
> But Little Lord Jesus, no crying he makes . . .

Mom?

"What?"

Wessel, y'know, he said this funny thing—

"*Who?*"

Jack Wessel! At church? He said— Okay, would Jo be, like, what they call . . . a "lesbian"?

"Steven! We *never* say that about *anyone*! It's a terrible thing to say, and I don't want to hear another *word* about it. I thought we just agreed that this isn't the time to go into this!"

She began cutting the crumpled edge from a smooth piece of paper. "We can at least rescue part of this." Suddenly she stopped and stared out the window. Her face had that look again, like at McDonald's, like someone was dying.

I looked down and sorted paper real hard. Mom got up and went into the dining room. I heard her whispering, like she was angry [*imitates his mother, furiously whispering, ascending to a frustrated squeak, as though about to cry*], but I couldn't hear what she was saying. I sat perfectly still. I thought, if I were a better boy, I'd go see what was the matter. But I didn't.

A minute later, she came back, smiling: "How about some cocoa?"

Sure! Then a crash came from overhead.

"Oh, *Russell!*" She took off upstairs. I heard her striding down the upstairs hall. Then she got all exasperated and Russell was saying something. Then more questions.

Then suddenly, everything was quiet, except for the radio. She acted like she was so mad at Russell, but she'd rather be with him, with his big nails.

I hopped up, tensed my muscles, and went to the window. I didn't deserve to be my parents' son or Jo's friend. I ran away from Jo, when she was just trying to help. Would they ever let me go and tell her I was sorry? I'd noticed, there were certain people we *weren't* sorry for doing certain things to. Or saying. Jo had to be thanked for Christmas presents, but we didn't worry if she felt bad about any of what had happened.

I wanted to climb out the window and go to Coe Hill and have it always be just two days before Christmas—Jo was right; that was the best time—and the two of us baking and gathering holly and pine. It couldn't be real. I couldn't be real. I tried hard to see past my reflection.

Finally, I turned back to our living room. Jo had her own life—dusting snow off her car, coming in for hot cider and a leftover by-cracky bar, Moose sitting up, begging for crumbs. Missing her and wanting to say I was sorry seemed like another present. One I would never open.

I hopped over to my real presents. Mom had moved Jo's "popsicle stick" when I tried on my sweater. Now it lay on top of a book from Dad, *The Real Diary of a Real Boy*. That's what it was! A bookmark!

JO: "So you'll always know where you are."

For the first and only time, the two actors' eyes meet. The NARRATOR looks away again before speaking.

NARRATOR: Thanks, Jo. I'm sorry about Sunday. I hope I see you soon. And Moose. I thought I was going to cry. I was afraid Mom would come back and ask what was the matter, and I was afraid she wouldn't.

I sat down again with the milk chocolate balls. With my little fingernails, I picked the foil off one and ate it. As soon as it was gone, I took another.

I sat in the empty living room with the choir singing, and I ate one chocolate ball after another, promising myself that each one would be the last.

As the NARRATOR mimes eating, the voice of a middle-aged woman, unseen by the audience (this may be recorded or live), sings the first verse of the folk song "The Parting Glass." Then a beat. The NARRATOR still mimes eating. The stage goes dark.

End of play.

November Door

for Donna Allegra

Just before Thanksgiving, 1995. The living/dining room of JO's apartment, on the second floor of a 1920s frame house, in the same town where The Snow Queen *took place. Worn furniture, some of it antique, including a dining table and chairs. Antique china, lamps, and rugs in middling condition. Painted New England scenes of no particular distinction. A receiver and speakers a decade out of date; a scattering of books (some very old) and magazines. A door frame with no door, stage left. It is past midnight. Lights low. Faintly we hear, as an instrumental, the hymn "This Is My Father's World."*

STEVEN [*unseen, at the back of the audience*]: The first night she woke at one a.m. and came to the south window, where she had managed to fit her mother's writing desk. She felt his presence before she saw him. She gazed down into the dim yellow light. From the other side of the street, in the shadows of the Olde Towne Condominiums, once Philip Trumbull Elementary, named for a Revolutionary War hero, he looked up. Was he, in fact, looking up at her? If not, why was he there? The house shuddered in the November wind.

She sat at the table. Not the big, old one, where she'd sat for years, years ago, years lived with her family, then by herself, in the house on Coe Hill. No, she'd had to sell that one, along with the house. She'd bought this one in Pennsylvania, to fit the smaller house there, near her brother, Dan, who had said,

"You can come here" in a voice that really said, "If you must." Now, she had made that table fit this apartment, back in the town where she was born. Safe. Sound. Somehow out of place, but she had wanted so much to return. Had felt it. Was drawn. She got up and looked again. Still there. Who the gee willikers—? A gust rattled the window. [*Sings.*] Good King Wenceslas looked out, on the feast of *Steven-with-a-v-not-a-p-h!*

The business . . . the *incident* with the young lady. The young lady from where she *worked*, where she was *responsible,* and so that was that. Love? Of course. Innocent seeming. And not. Transgression had been part of the gratification. And she was ever so suitably put out of the family home. The academy fired her and then "agreed" to buy it. Twenty-some years as their carpenter. The young lady's father, a judge, no less, would not press matters, so long as she moved away. And so her brother, reluctant Wenceslas, found her a home near Lancaster. She told neither him nor his wife the full story. "There must have been some misunderstanding," he said brusquely. "I would say they misunderstood a great many things," she sighed. She never used a pronoun for Clara. She spoke, if she had to, of "the student" or "the person." Dan and his wife echoed her.

Years later, she woke one day and had to return— and decided she could. She came back and went around, and she didn't know anyone and no one seemed to know her. The couple here showed her their second floor. They mispronounced the names of parks and roads and didn't know where neighboring towns were. They certainly hadn't heard of the incident. Or of her. Why would they? Whatever they thought, they all signed a lease. In the dark he looked up and thought, *This is it. She who, in my childhood, lived in the impossibly vast house on Coe Hill, who had a music room and a whole kingdom of meadows and woods . . . She is here, renting. Maybe because of me. What I did. And said. Would she know me today?* [*Sings.*] Yonder peasant, who is he, where and what his dwelling?

Blackout. Lights come up low as before. Another verse of "This Is My Father's World."

STEVEN: The second night she woke and came out again.

It seemed he looked right up into her eyes. In the morning she'd call Fred Thompson on the town police force and ask him to take a swing by the next night. This person was harming no one, but . . . She'd built cabinets for Fred last year. Put a crick in her back. Sixty-five now. She felt the years and the contradictions. She could not get back to sleep.

JO exits. Blackout. Lights up again, a bit brighter.

The third night she did not have to wait. [*STEVEN comes down the aisle and stops at the edge of the stage.*] Footsteps came up the outside stairs. One of the church people, stopping on some pretext? Dalton, with his lisp and his limp, who wore the same blue-and-orange-striped shirt each week. Paul, from the lumberyard, stopping by after his meeting. Lost ones. Having lost the family house on Coe Hill, she was one of them. Where was home, now, for anyone?

STEVEN comes up onstage and goes to the door frame stage left. He knocks.

JO: Who is it?

STEVEN: An old friend, I guess.

JO: Which old friend?

STEVEN: From long ago. [*BOTH have their right ears cocked on their respective sides of the door frame, so they face in opposite directions, inches apart, the imaginary door between them.*]

JO: I know a lot of people from long ago.

STEVEN: "Emergency cider run!"

JO: What? [*She cracks the door. STEVEN stares at her and she at him.*] Do I know you?

STEVEN: Not anymore, I guess. I bet—

JO: Well, maybe you had better stop guessing. It's late and I—

STEVEN: I'm sorry. I'm sorry. I—

JO: What is your name? You're the one who's been down there for two, three nights now, looking up at me. What for? Hm. You don't know that, either. Or your own name!

STEVEN: Oh, I know what my tax return and my driver's license say. I just can't connect it anymore.

JO: Well, then, what the heck, maybe I'd better have a look at that driver's license, if— Do you need medical help?

STEVEN: I do need help.

JO: You look exhausted. Are you ill?

STEVEN: No, not the way you're thinking.

JO: So, ill some other way? You get a conk on the head and—?

STEVEN: No, no . . .

JO: You do look familiar. At my age, everyone looks familiar. [*She looks at the license.*] Underwood. Steven. The Underwoods on . . . You helped me with chores! You were one of the boys from church. My dad delivered you. Of course. Would you like to come in? [*He nods and steps in.*] Good Lord, you do look, um, winded. Are you hungry? Steven, should I be worried?

STEVEN: Oh, no! Please—

JO: Take off your coat. [*STEVEN does.*] Sit down. I have some tea, and I have some shortbreads.

STEVEN: Oh, my God!

JO: What? What is it?

STEVEN: You still have shortbreads. Maybe they will help.

JO: Help what?

STEVEN: My "illness." No no, it isn't anything. Not like you're thinking.

JO: All right . . . well . . . Steven Underwood. [*STEVEN smiles.*] Spying on me outside my window? What for? You could have just rung me up! What brings you back here? You don't live hereabouts anymore, do you? [*STEVEN shakes his head.*] Your mother sold the house on—was it Weldon Ave.? [*STEVEN nods. JO sits next to him and takes his hand.*] I was sorry to hear about your dad's death. That was just after I came back. Here. I didn't go to the funeral. Didn't know them all that well, I suppose. My dad delivered you, though.

STEVEN: I remember.

JO: So, what brings you back, looking up at my window in the middle of the night?

STEVEN: My mother's sick.

JO: Oh. Oh, I'm very sorry to hear that.

STEVEN: It's nothing too serious. She lives at Rush Glen in Bloomfield. The retirement community?

JO: I know it.

STEVEN: I was the one who could take the time off. My brother would never do it. [*Looks around the room.*]

JO: Well, you tell her she has my best wishes. Give me her address, and I'll write a card. [*Pause.*] What is it?

STEVEN: All the things I remember. All of them in the wrong place.

JO: What wrong place?

STEVEN: Not on Coe Hill. Let's go up to Coe Hill!

JO: Beg pardon?

STEVEN: Right now! In your truck. I passed it when—

JO: Why?

STEVEN: No reason, I guess. Stupid.

JO: It's too late, for one thing.

STEVEN: Yeah. Someone else lives there.

JO: No, I meant late at *night*. Listen, you still haven't told me how you've been! Gosh, it's been twenty-some years. Last time I saw you must have been, oh, let me see, the summer I redid the robing room. Yes.

STEVEN: No.

JO: Well, good of you to come back, take care of your mom. Now, what are you up to?

STEVEN: The last time was that November. After— After you knew you had to leave, and we hadn't seen each other for—

JO: Oh, well—

STEVEN: —a while. I came up to Coe Hill.

JO: That's all water over the bridge. *Under* the bridge. *Over* the dam. Brain's going! At any rate, I don't think about it anymore. But *you*—

STEVEN: You had to give up the house you were born in.

JO: Well, as I said—

STEVEN: I felt responsible.

JO: Responsible? You?

STEVEN: Because I told them. The dean. At the academy. About *her*. Clara. Being at your house . . .

JO: I remember. They extracted some information from you. Information they already knew, I'm sure. You needn't feel bad, Steven. They wouldn't have asked you if they hadn't already suspected that certain things had, you know, transpired. Academies are the opposite of the law. The law can know, but they have to prove. The academy—they don't even have to know. It only mattered what they *thought*. And . . . yes, they did think . . . somewhat correctly. And just tricked you into confirming. Took advantage of you. But no. No no no. No more bad feelings. Over the dam. I do remember that day, though. The light almost gone. Leaves gone. You were in a little bit of a state. But not anymore. I honestly don't know what anyone would have done differently. [*Rises.*] Let's get some tea going.

STEVEN: Like we did after chores, up on—

JO: Yes, yes! You know, it was actually time I got out of the Old Manse. Almost a relief, you know, to sell and be done with it. The taxes alone! The academy always wanted it. And then . . . Pennsylvania, lived near my brother, Dan, found a church, sang. Wasn't *home* home, but it was fine. I worried at first. Someone would find out. Someone from there would have a second cousin from here, and they—

STEVEN: Oh, Jo . . . !

JO: I didn't tell Dan or his wife everything. Then one day—maybe in the kitchen or out back with the— I suddenly realized, I wasn't worrying! I was *more* home.

STEVEN: But not *home* home.

JO [*shaking her head a little*]: Have you seen it, by the way? The house? The academy bought it, you know, along with the land. They'd been offering for years. They made it very nice. I wanted them to name it "Osbourne House," after Dad. He was the school physician for twenty years, you know, but apparently the name "Osbourne" was all of a sudden . . . a bit "tricky." Thanks to me. Sorry, Dad. But it helped me get the place in Pennsylvania. The young lady grew up and left. We haven't, of course, you know, had any . . . contact. Her father retired in eighty-eight? Nine? People forget. Many never even knew. I was afraid to go back to church, but everyone just said, "Where have you been? It's wonderful to see you!" Even academy people act like they don't know. And I had to be where I was born. Had to at least try. [*Squeezes STEVEN's hand perfunctorily; seems to notice something about it.*] So, if that's what you came about, do not you worry. Everything turned out fine. Now, tell me what's been happening with you! You know, I remember those Saturday afternoons quite fondly.

STEVEN: Sundays!

JO: Yes. *Sundays.*

STEVEN: Until—

JO: Raking leaves and cleaning the basement, if I recall, and . . . didn't we cut holly at Christmas?

STEVEN: Until—

JO: I remember thinking you'd be an author or an

actor or—. [*Chuckles, pats his hand again.*] I don't know what I'm saying.

STEVEN: Until my parents ruined it.

JO: Well, I did let time get away from us a few times. You get out there, where there is no time, almost, and you want— They just lived a different way, your folks. They were worried about you! [*Looks at STEVEN.*] And to tell you the truth, I'm a little bit worried, too. Excuse my saying so, but you look awfully drawn. [*Pause.*] I have to ask that question again, a little more seriously, about you being ill. I mean, *are* you, in some way—? [*STEVEN nods.*] Oh. I see. Oh, dear. Oh, dear.

STEVEN: What? Oh, no. No, it isn't that! Jeez, I wish it was. Almost.

JO: Wait . . . No, don't say that. What is it?

STEVEN: Not that kind of illness. I told you.

JO: Well, *what* kind of illness?

STEVEN [*hesitates, then indicates his heart*]: Here. I guess. Here [*indicating his head*]. I don't know where it lives. [*Long pause.*] Jo, I drove to Bloom-field from where I live in New Jersey. Three days ago. On the way, I stopped. At every single rest stop on the highway. The whole way.

JO: I see. So [*patting her midriff*], here. Or wherever the kidneys actually are. My dad may have been a doctor, but I—

STEVEN: No! I was *looking*. At each and every one. *Searching*. Didn't *do* anything, really, but—

JO: Oh. I see. Yes, I think I do.

STEVEN: Took me God knows how long to get here! Six hours, for a three-hour trip? I kept calling my mother and saying there was a traffic jam.

JO: Well, that is a sobering thing to hear.

STEVEN: And, like I said, it's not like I did anything. Please, please don't think— Any of that. I just waited. And wanted. And despaired. Finally slammed the car in gear and thought how great the next one would be. But, over the years, sometimes . . . in, you know, a bar, or . . . at those rest stops . . . I thought if I could just get away, *away* from wherever I was, *who*ever I was, whoever I'd turned into, back to Coe Hill. One of those afternoons, just before Christmas or in fall. The light going. But those after-noons ended.

BOTH fall silent for a time.

JO: Moose died, you know. There. My pup.

STEVEN: I'm sorry.

JO: For a time I swore I still heard his nails on the floor. [*Pause.*] You know, I had a friend, when I was young. Must have been the late forties, here in town. Jimmie Christopher. You have any old Broadway records, he's on a couple of them, in the fine print. Chorus. After he went there, New York, he wrote to me. He never talked about— Not directly, anyway. My dad called him a "sad case." Well-meaning, of course, but— Anyway, he wrote, Jimmie did, and he said once, "There are places here that people like me can go, to *have fun.*"

STEVEN: Yeah. There are. "Fun." I just want to be back on Coe Hill. *Then.*

JO: I know. Fond memories. That aren't coming back. That can't. They help us through, though. Is there someone you can talk to? [*Pause.*] Where you live, I mean. You're more than welcome here.

STEVEN: There was. But he . . . left. Maybe I wanted him to. I sent him away. I couldn't give him what he was here, on Earth, for. And no one seems to— He looked at me with these big eyes, and I almost hated him for it. After, I tried to hold him and apologize. Finally, someone would make a joke. We'd watch TV and pretend it was okay. But he wanted—needed— something else and something else, the way people do, I guess. He never knew about my "hobby," of course. No, it really is a job. One I don't want, but it just takes you. "Hires" you. Searching. For what your friend searched for, what I was— It's a job. Hey, you remember the Kale Gods?

JO: I'm sorry?

STEVEN: "Sacrificing the Sacred Peanut-Butter Cookie to the Kale Gods!"

JO: Was this something you and I used to do—? Because I do remember making—

STEVEN: I helped you plant your garden, one Sunday. And you said, to make the garden grow, we had to "sacrifice the Sacred Peanut-Butter Cookie to the Kale Gods."

JO: Well, that sounds like me.

STEVEN: Which basically meant we ate it. The

cookies. And there was the "ancient chant" that went with it: "Oh-wa! Ta-goo! Siam!"

JO [*laughs*]: Oh, yes, that I remember. From Camp Wildwood. Don't say it too loud today! And I'm sure we did plant kale. But, Steven, you'll have to forgive me, I've forgotten so much of Coe Hill. I threw out a lifetime. Several lifetimes. Mother and Dad, too. The guilt! *Their house, empty.* In Pennsylvania, sometimes, I stood at the sink, at dusk, and I looked at strange woods and wondered, was *it* lonely? The house. Did it miss me? How did it look, at that moment? Where was the sun? I got the *Academy Bulletin*: "Dedication of—" Whatever they named it instead of "Osbourne House." Sorry, Dad. [*This stops her for a moment.*] So sorry. [*STEVEN takes her hand. She squeezes it, then takes it away.*] And I moved on, and now, back in town. Building bookcases for folks, fixing plumbing. You know what I do. At any rate, this "illness" business, now. Please, tell me something about it? Do you work? Or do you—?

STEVEN: Oh, no. Not to worry. I have a job. I have insurance. I'm a kind of glorified assistant/receptionist at this arts center. Out in the wilds of New Jersey, across from the City. I can see where your friend— Those places, basically. It's funny you said an author or an actor. Before, I worked for a community college, and I took a writing course at night. First time, felt like a whole new life beginning. But when I was alone and put pen to paper, these voices—not real ones, thank God!—said, "No, you're not one of those people." The Assured. The Elected. Voices like whole novels. Anti-novels. You struggle with a real story—I mean, you think it's real—and underneath, these voices are reciting volume after volume of defeat. That's genius. Those voices are geniuses. Our destruction is their masterpiece.

JO: I think many of us feel that way at one time or another. Why we need to be geniuses, though—

STEVEN: After he was asleep, I'd look out and think, I was supposed to be good. I was supposed to be good and do things. I did publish one poem.

JO: Really? Where?

STEVEN: Nowhere.

JO: Might I hear it?

STEVEN [*after a pause*]: I don't have it memorized. I didn't like it that much.

JO: Why?

STEVEN: It's about my family and it's not "forgiving." Don't geniuses forgive? You always forgave. "Water over the dam," right? I pass the church where I live and can't even look. Being a "Christian" would suffocate me. If God had anything to say to me, which He never did. Sunday school was always just, "Underwood's a faggot, pass it on." Jesus wouldn't let them stone the adulteress or whoever, but me? Us? Whatever. He didn't say about that. He didn't have to. He knew that, one day, legions of blond, athletic Protestant Sunday school boys would do it for Him. [*Looks at JO.*] I'm sorry.

JO: No trouble. I suppose He's strong enough to hear it! Steven: I don't think God is some kind of dictator. I'm hardly the expert. Nor, of course, does he always help us along the way we might like.

STEVEN: I know.

JO: We can't worry about what other people have or what they do. Inside they might be starving, like kids from Biafra. They might be sitting in front of a heaping plate of food saying, "I don't want it!" Or they might not. We might ask them to teach us. As for forgiving, truly, what else is there to do?

STEVEN: Oh, there's plenty else—

JO: —that's not going to change anyone, or anything that happened. You have to find the good.

STEVEN: Please!

JO: I am serious. There is truly nothing else to do. Of course, there is that ache, once in a while. They say that would go away if I accepted Christ as my personal Lord and Savior. I talk about water over and under things, but the kind of acceptance they mean there—I guess I'm like a horse that gets right up to the whatever-you-call-it and won't leap. Always went at everything *my* way. Slant. But I have a sense of God watching. And understanding. And if life isn't always "good"—and it ain't sometimes, and I literally could not tell you that at ten or eleven, but you know now! So, *when* it isn't good, it does still make a kind of . . . inexplicable sense.

STEVEN: Not to me!

JO: And that sense embraces us. A unwritten, unpronounceable language for understanding yourself.

For changing, a little. For accepting. A lot! Which is an art and ultimately a satisfying one. Like carpentry. Maybe when you go away and chase a destiny, you stand alone up there in the Arctic and ask, Why *am* I as I am? You thought you could do anything. And where was God the whole time, and why does He seem to love that one over there more? I went to visit Jimmie once, in New York. The train stalled in New Haven. I missed the show. I pretty much had to turn around and come back, I thought.

STEVEN: The Pennsylvania thing must have been awful.

JO: There, you see? It wasn't! I was near my brother. It was fine. What did you go away for, Mr. Underwood? In particular.

STEVEN: Oh, I just assumed. I went to the nice little New England college that my parents— Well, that my mother wanted. And to be fair, I did, too. It felt safe. It's what everyone wanted. I didn't think, then. And I had this friend there, in college. Just a friend. He came from New Jersey, near where I am now. He said, when we graduated, we'd go there and share an apartment. Get jobs. Like college, only— And he'd never had a girlfriend and never talked about getting one, and I found that reassuring. So we graduated and off we went. I got the job at the community college. And that first summer, suddenly, one day, there was a girl around. Perfectly nice girl. Woman. Young woman. And we were all friends. Three Musketeers! Then one day it was, "Didn't I tell you? Debbie and I are—" Going to such-and-such a place. "We didn't think you'd be interested." Then, it was all the time. When he moved in with her, I was stunned. And not surprised at all. I got a stranger for a roommate. And [*gesturing toward himself*] Steven went to their place for dinner. Steven went to their wedding. Didn't usher, though. He had better friends. All of whom brought girlfrie— Well, brought girls. And they flew away. Would you believe—I thought of moving back *here*? For two seconds. But the reason most people would move back was the reason I didn't: people here know me. So I stayed where I was. And I came to know other people . . . who had never been back to their towns.

JO: And I don't understand that! Someone rejecting the place they were born. Someone who no longer responds to that angle of light. That person, I think, is lost. [*STEVEN gives her a look.*] I'm sorry, but I do. Not permanently.

STEVEN: So why *didn't* you "accept Jesus Christ as your Lord and Savior"?

JO: Well, as I said, I am used to doing things my own way. Didn't want the sympathy. Around here, they don't really ask what you believe. How about you?

STEVEN: How about me, what?

JO: The church. And you.

STEVEN: Well, no one in my family ever *believed* anything. They thought it was unseemly to have faith. One knew things, the more the better, and adults had "a right to their opinion." But faith, belief, redemption? A God with good manners doesn't pry like that. Look, I'm sorry, it's late.

JO: You're sorry it's late?

STEVEN [*rising*]: I think I overstayed my welcome.

JO: No!

STEVEN: I didn't even give you a chance to welcome me or not. Just walked up.

JO: Well, I'm glad you did!

STEVEN: I'd better get back to Bloomfield.

JO: Where did you park?

STEVEN: Oh. I . . . didn't park. I didn't bring the car. I walked . . .

JO: Walked? From Bloomfield? Good Lord!

STEVEN: It was beautiful. The journey. Everything dark, slowly passing.

JO: All three nights? [*STEVEN nods.*] Because I saw you out there. Well, at least let me drive you back. I'll get dressed.

STEVEN: No, please. [*Looks around the room.*]

JO: Of course I will! Good heavens, it's after midnight!

STEVEN: I just can't go quite yet.

JO: I don't understand.

STEVEN: I can't leave yet. You. Here. All the times I came to your house on Coe Hill, all those afternoons, the sun going down, I wished something would happen, some emergency, a blizzard, a cozy emergency, and I'd have to stay. I could go to sleep with the grandfather clock and the dried herbs in the kitchen, watching. I thought they stayed awake at night, and they'd—

JO: Would you like to stay? Here? And now?

STEVEN: Oh, no! I didn't mean that! Look, I've imposed enough.

JO: Not at all!

STEVEN: Plus, all that lurking downstairs. That must have been an imposition.

JO: No matter. Stay, Steven. I have an extra room. The bed's all made up. Then I'll drive you over in the morning. [*Beat.*] It's what you came for, isn't it?

STEVEN: Yes.

JO: Well, then.

STEVEN: But you shouldn't. You—

JO: Do you have to call your mother and let her know?

STEVEN: No. They have guest rooms there that family and friends stay in. So I already said goodnight. Long time ago.

JO: Well, then, I think it's settled. You'll be right in there. I'll get some towels.

JO disappears, then reappears with towels and a comforter and gives them to STEVEN. He takes them.

STEVEN: Thanks.

JO: Bathroom's back around there. I put out a toothbrush, from the dentist. I have about a dozen!

BOTH stand in silence a moment.

STEVEN: I always wished I could stay. All the afternoons of chores had to end.

JO: Once or twice, I didn't get you home on time.

STEVEN: How safe it was. I thought, if I fell asleep there, I'd wake up in some olden time, and I'd be a good boy and would go out and conquer the world and come home to Coe Hill.

JO: You were a very good boy. To me.

STEVEN: Oh, no!

JO: And I thought about it, too. Having you over. But there are things you try. And things you know not to.

STEVEN: That girl. Clara. She got to stay over.

JO [*after some consideration*]: Different.

STEVEN: I know. I'm sorry.

JO: I thought no one saw. And that was the thing: they didn't. You can do so much, and no one sees. Or they choose not to see. And then, one time, one thing, that's the day they choose. To see and see. Things that might be there, things that might not be. The world . . . flips. You're told to leave your home. Or you're the one who doesn't see. Presto, your friend is married. How many years was he your friend? You knew. I knew. I befriended someone who, I thought, needed it. Whose father— You know, he stood there, at the end, with this look of disgust on his face. But I had been in love. Like you. And not for the first time.

Silence.

STEVEN: It's not right, you letting me stay.

JO: You always wanted it, and now, I give it to you. I'll drive you back in the morning. Have to go to the lumberyard anyway.

STEVEN: Well, thank you.

JO: You are very welcome. Good night. I'm so glad you came.

Pause. JO exits. Lights fade to very dim. STEVEN undresses and brings the chair he was sitting in downstage center, to stand for a bed. If the stage is big enough, there can be a separate guest room area, with a twin bed. He curls up under the comforter.

STEVEN: He lay awake trying to grasp and hold on to how the years of wishing and pretending had ended. But he was not snug. This artificial— It would end, too, just hours from now, and he'd go, again, for the last time, maybe. He did not belong here. Neither did she. Better people slept on Coe Hill now, its vast, dim rooms small and bright, all smooth, windows soundlessly sliding shut. Sealed. Poor Jo. Her presence in the next room did not make him feel safe, as it once would have. As he once thought it would have. A car passed in the street. That made him feel safe. Life had given him enough for him to hope another little while.

He tried to stay awake, holding, holding on to the years and at the same time altering them. In the end, it collapsed, his brain a muddle. He tried to now. That now, finally, he lay under her comforter; now, just now, her curtains brushed his face. But he was tired, and he fell asleep.

Softly a hymn plays. A solo voice sings low. JO enters, stands center stage. The music continues under her monologue. STEVEN stirs and twitches in his sleep.

JO: A billion to three hundred million years ago, across the surface of the Earth, tectonic plates collided and stuck together, forming a single continent, stretching from the North Pole to the South. Near the Equator, the ocean rock formed that would one day underlie the state of Connecticut.

STEVEN [*in his sleep, soft but petulant, whiny*]: I don't want it! No, I don't want it!

JO: The one continent stretched, and the land dropped. The Hartford Basin formed, which runs up through central Connecticut, into Massachusetts. Lake muds and stream gravel came down from the hills and filled the valley as it was forming.

Two hundred and ninety million years ago, volcanic eruptions across the continent caused ninety-eight percent of everything alive on land or in the oceans to die.

Twenty million years passed before life diversified again.

STEVEN [*as before, here and there, sparingly, through the next four paragraphs*]: No, no, I don't want it!

JO: Two hundred and twenty-five million years ago,

fractures opened in the Earth's surface, running up from New Haven to Deerfield, Mass. Lava poured up at Higganum, New Haven, and Hamden, forming ridges of basalt, or "trap rock." [*Pointing.*] You see the Hamden Basalt just west of here, where the Farmington River cuts through the Tariffville Gorge.

During the three hundred thousand years between the New Haven and Hamden lava flows, lakes formed on top of existing basalt. Lake sediment covered the basalts as deep as six thousand feet, up here where Interstate 91 runs through. These solidi-fied into "Portland arkose," or "brownstone," which thins as you travel this way.

A hundred and ninety million years ago, the one continent began to break apart, and the Atlantic Ocean opened up. Sixty-five million years ago, a comet or asteroid, perhaps as wide as a mile and a half, struck the Earth in the Yucatán. Seventy-five percent of everything alive on land or in the oceans died, including dinosaurs.

The continent continued to break up, and Connecti-cut moved northward. A drop in the level of carbon dioxide marked the beginning of the modern ice age, two million years ago. Ice sheets advanced, rounding the Connecticut hills and filling the valleys with sediment, mud, and gravel.

The hymn ends about here.

STEVEN: [*as before, here and there through the next two paragraphs*]: No, I don't want it!

JO: The first humans lived along the edge of the

glacial ice, where they hunted migrating reindeer, mastodon, and bison. The last ice sheets receded from Connecticut 14,000 years ago, and the Farmington and Connecticut Rivers assumed their present forms, flowing through the glacial sediments and following the paths of the older earth structures.

Indian tribes, including the Mohegan, Niantic, and Pequot, occupied what would become the State of Connecticut. Today, their languages have all been lost.

STEVEN [*as before*]: I'm sick. I'm sick.

JO: In 1633, an English trader, William Holmes, sailed up the Connecticut River, past Hartford, and landed here. In 1637, a court in Hartford authorized an "offensive war" against the Pequots.

In 1783, the town, though pressed hard by war, sent 21,115 pounds of beef to the Continental Army.

March 1, 1784—Connecticut, home to more slaves than any other New England state, passed an act of Gradual Abolition.

In 1894, citizens of the town formed a whist club and a marching band.

STEVEN: I don't. No.

JO: December 25, 1942. Dad gave me this diary for Christmas. I love its blank, white pages. It's dark out now, down to twenty degrees, and little flakes of snow twirl down outside Dad's study. [*STEVEN stirs and makes more noises.*] Danny says there will be a blizzard. The war goes on. Dad was upset about a

Frenchman assassinated in Algeria, and there was a mudslide in Pennsylvania.

July 18, 1943. Mother is sick again. I waved to her from the garden. I was gathering zucchini, and I stopped and prayed for her.

STEVEN [*writhes, eyes shut, conducts a dialogue between himself and a long-ago schoolmate*]: "Hey, Underwood, lemme ask you a question. You consider yourself a normal guy?" "What's that mean?" "No, just, do you consider yourself a normal guy? I'm doing a survey." "I guess so." "You consider yourself normal guy." "Yeah." "So . . . next question: how come your best friend's a lesbo?"

Pause.

JO: March 8, 1945. We think Mother is better. Dad's crocuses have come up. Croc-*i*, he would say. I believe I saw a phoebe this morning. I thanked God for it. The way I'm supposed to. The Allies are crossing the Rhine. I hope the war ends soon.

Dad sent the money for Camp Wildwood this summer. I don't know what to think of it. I don't know what to think of anything, sometimes. What if I go and Mother—

STEVEN [*a bull session between schoolmates*]: "You think it's, like, sexual?" "Oh, gross!" "No, seriously, you think he, like, *fucks* her?" "Naw, she fucks him!" "She's one of your turbo-charged lesbo types. They got dicks!" "Oh, man, lesbo-dick, I'm gonna vomit!" [*Fake vomiting noise, hysterical laughter.*]

JO: April 30, 1946. Mother died this morning. I cut daffodils for the funeral. I hope she was not . . . disappointed in me. Dad said, "You *will* wear a dress." And I did. [*Pause.*] The valley turns green. More and more. I look out and see. Yesterday I saw an oriole, back early. October 14, 1948. Coming home on the bus from Hartford I saw horse chestnuts under the Knowleses' tree. Shiny when they come from the pod. I keep them in my room, and they shrivel and darken. They are like old wood or stone. I have one for every year. [*Pause.*] He swore at me.

STEVEN [*as a college buddy*]: "Underwood, man, it's just biology. You go up to a chick at one of these parties and you just say, 'Hey, how 'bout a little biology?' We all want the same thing, right?"

JO: March 30, 1950. I look down, thinking how safe and cozy people are in the valley, wondering if I will ever live there.

STEVEN [*as the friend with whom he moved in after college*]: "Her name's Debbie. She's nice. You'll like her. We'll go out some time. Three Musketeers!"

JO: January 1, 1952. Dan left for New Haven this morning. Dark and ice in the afternoon. Walked out as far as the stone wall. I thought I saw a wolf, but you doubt yourself.

STEVEN [*as a mannered, bitchy acquaintance*]: "Okay, this is *awful*. Stevie, listen up! God's making Adam and Eve. And he's got them all done except the genitals. So he's got Adam and Eve and he's got the two sets of genitals—Stevie, *listen!*—and he turns to Saint Peter and says, 'Okay, which one goes on which?' And Saint Peter says, 'Oh, give the dumb one the cunt!'"

JO: September 10, 1956. Dad sick again. I don't like to see him lying there. I try to pray. Nighthawks have come, and some blackbirds. The hawks follow the river. We watched Elvis Presley on *The Ed Sullivan Show*. I didn't know what to think. It seems I never do.

STEVEN: "Normal, straight-looking guy seeks same, 25 to 35 max for friendship and possible LTR. You are open, outgoing, in good shape but not a gym bunny. Not into games but into long walks, long talks, dining out, dancing, sports . . . and hot sex. You know George Sand and George Eliot were women but you don't make a point of telling everyone. You like to smile and share fun times. You could be the light of my life. [*Slight pause.*] Please be sane, d/d free. [*Slight pause.*] No fats/femmes."

JO: February 15, 1957. Dad died last night . . . February 28. I keep thinking, I should bring him toast or a pillow. Something happens and I think, I must tell Dad . . .

STEVEN [*voice of a sex personal*]: "Come by my place, the door'll be open, I'll be bent over displaying my soft girly ass. You unzip, drop trou, fuck me without a rubber, tell me what a girly ass I have, drop your load and go. Bi/straight/married a plus."

JO: October 25, 1967. Oak leaves dancing across Old Town Road. A Wilkinson girl broke from her friends and danced with them. [*Pause.*] Like a witch . . . They are so free. God is good. He doesn't look at me.

STEVEN [*as his ex*]: "Steven, you are the most haunted person I know! What's it about? When I talk to you and you make that face! You talk about these parents, I mean, they must have done some number on you! Come on, talk to me! Say anything! You always do this!"

JO: December 21, 1968. Steven U. here to help bake for church. Sang carols in the woods and collected holly for the house. Always the parents, watching.

STEVEN [*still as the ex*]: "It's not your fault, Steven. You did the best you could. I think you understand, I have to go. I have to take care of me. I hope you find the help you need." [*Pause. Under JO's next speech STEVEN quietly cries and repeats*:] "I don't know. Can't we—? Can't someone—? Help me? Help me!"

JO: July 18, 1976. Met a young woman, Clara, at church. Judge's daughter. Goes to the academy. I'd seen her. I think she seems to need someone . . . August 8. Clara, here. I taught her to put mint in iced tea. She seemed amazed, abashed, maybe, that you could just pick leaves from the garden and put them in your tea and have what other people have, I guess. [*Pause.*] August 11. Clara . . . August 21. Clara, late. Her dad does not treat her well. I should do something. To stop it . . . [*Long pause.*] September 30. Called to the Head's office about C. Surprise. The judge was there. Looking at me like some— Like I was both evil and not even there. What could I say? Everything and nothing. November 2. C's father— I don't feel like writing tonight. [*Pause.*] Dad gave me my first diary when I was twelve. November 25. Sold my home, Dad's and Mother's, mine, to the academy.

An hour and it was done. They have horse chestnuts and stone walls in other places. And young women like C. November 28. Steven U. came. Distraught about my going. He believes it is his fault. They took advantage of him. He is protecting something in himself. Each of us has their way. I keep thinking it's, well, I hate to say it—poor character. But no. I think this would have happened— What is "character"? Doing what everyone else wants? No . . . Guarding something in himself. Something we don't ask for. Something no one asks about.

April 2, 1989. Back in town, living upstairs in what used to be the Rices' house on Bidwell Ave. May 14, 1989. Fixed some finials for the folks downstairs. They think I'm a miracle worker! Have some bookcases and a TV table on order, too. [*Pause.*] December 29, 1993. Mockingbirds overwinter here now. Woodpeckers, too. Down to fifteen last night.

Home.

JO pauses, exits. Lights begin to fade up very slowly, brighter than before. STEVEN wakes, stretches.

STEVEN: When he woke, he felt for the first time in years as though he were waking *at home.* But it wasn't. The sun was rising, rituals were running out, and he would go. Maybe he wanted to, the impossible being done. He looked through the dusty window at November grass, scrubby, brown, enduring. Bare branches. The street and the traffic signs weren't the endless woods and valley over which he would have looked from Coe Hill, had he ever been allowed to wake in her real house. The sun touched a curtain. If he stayed perfectly still beneath the blanket, her knock would never come. [*JO knocks. STEVEN gets up and starts to dress.*] And the leaf-plastered sidewalk would become mist extending to the horizon, years ago, punctuated as it went by steeples.

JO [*knocking again*]: Mr. U? I have some breakfast, if you'd like.

STEVEN: Okay! The Lord gave a mockery of dreams, and the Lord took it away and left what was only real.

STEVEN comes into the main room. JO sets out coffee and muffins. BOTH sit. STEVEN eats. JO sips coffee.

STEVEN: Tastes the same.

JO: It should!

STEVEN: I make them sometimes. Not like yours.

JO: You make muffins?

STEVEN: I think, when they're done, I'll be somewhere else. There'll be a moment, when I'm mixing them. When they go into the oven. When I put them in the basket, or when I take the first one and eat. A moment before I swallow and it's gone. Then I think of when I will make them again. They'll be different. I made by-cracky bars once. Remember by-cracky bars?

JO: Sure! Still make 'em, occasionally. Mostly for other people.

STEVEN: I had to guess. I burned one corner a little.

JO: Oh, one must! Not homemade if you don't. Steven, where will you go? [*STEVEN looks at her.*] After this. Metaphorically speaking. [*HE seems distressed.*] What is it?

STEVEN: Well, I'm on this little sabbatical, from the arts center. I mean, it's fine. They suggested it. Just two weeks. I'd been a little . . . tired, you know. Erratic, maybe. Just two weeks. I'll pull it all together, I'll go home. Actually, if never metaphorically. Funny, this feels like it should be home.

JO: It is. You just can't stay. [*STEVEN nods.*]

STEVEN: The first three days I did nothing but read. Slept right there on the couch. I'm on this science and math kick, of all things. I realized I had no idea how the world works. So I started reading everything I could get my hands on. I've bought more books on the subject than I can read or afford.

JO: You dad was a math teacher.

STEVEN: And I think about someone. Then I think about what it would turn into. Something was amputated. It can't be that he's never coming back. One morning, I took the train to Hoboken; wound up on the promenade. Seeking, seeking. I looked across the river, at the City. How did those people get those lives? You're just going to tell me to look for the good.

JO: Well?

STEVEN: Well, either, a) I can't; or b) I don't believe it'd do any good. I'm not one of those people who can—

JO: The world doesn't care what you believe.

STEVEN: It just seems less and less worth dreaming.

JO: I'll tell you about dreams, Steven. I think that—
What do you call them? Graphs like this? [*She
traces the shape in the air.*]

STEVEN: Bell curves.

JO: You have the middle, and you have the ends.
You want things. And most people, most people you
and I know, God or whomever says yes and no in
pretty much equal measure. They're in the middle.
And to some people, He, She, I don't know, *seems* to
say yes almost all the time. And some people seem
to get, *seem* to get, mostly noes. Actually, when
people get a lot of noes, you know for sure. They're
right out there in the rain. Begging. Seeking. You
want to ask, Steven— And I know I'm not supposed
to say this. You want to ask for what you know
you're going to get a yes for. It's my dream that I
wake up this morning in the town where I was born,
and it's my dream to have some coffee and some of
my own hot biscuits. It's my dream that this week I'll
remodel a room for Ernie Cameron and his wife—
you remember the Camerons, the dad taught at the
high school, the mother died of leukemia? Ernie's—

STEVEN: I remember Ernie Cameron.

JO: The eldest, right, he built—

STEVEN: "Underwood's a femme, pass it on." I
remember Ernie Cameron. "Ooh, look, Underwood's
gonna cry. Maybe it's 'that time of the month'!" I
remember—

JO: Well, Ernie is grown up now. And the point is not Ernie. You hear things from kids when—

STEVEN: Maybe he was one of the ones who spray-painted your wall.

JO: Beg pardon?

STEVEN: Who spray-painted your stone wall that time. With you-know-what.

JO: Well, that's also water over or under something. At any rate, *whoever* I'm working for, it's my dream that I do the work for them, the best I know how. And then it is then my dream that I'll come home to some tea and a leftover biscuit, and sit by the window, maybe see a bird at the bird feeder. What kind of bird that is, I leave to— And it's my dream that when it gets dark I'll reread some Henry Beston or Edwin Way Teale, and it's my dream that I'll go to sleep under my mother's quilt. And I do.

STEVEN: It sounds like settling.

JO: It is a whole world of yeses, Steven. *My own* yeses. But no one can avoid the noes, of course. But think: One day I'm sawing in the garage out back, or hammering. And, um, God comes down the drive-way, out for a walk the way people do here, and He says, "Jo, I need you to make me a kitchen table. But, Jo, I'm sorry. I don't have any yeses for you to make that table with. I'm out of yeses, because I had to give them to some other folks. So, Jo, I need you to take some noes that I have. I need you to take those noes and make a table out of them. I know you can." What would I say? "I'd be happy to." And I'd take those noes and I'd make a table! I would and I have. And I tell you—

STEVEN [*grins*]: I have no idea what this is about.

JO: Yes, you do! And if He comes day after day, out on His walk, and every time He says, "Jo, I have some more noes for you." You say, "Thank you, I'll make another table." It doesn't mean you don't struggle. It means you do your job. *Your* job. And as you do it, as you make the table, you cut into a no, and a little bead pops out. A maybe. A row of them, following the grain. And you make a table. And the table—

STEVEN: I don't think you understand my life. I don't have any mission; I don't have any home. I gave up my home. On a big, stupid promise. Now I lie awake at night and long for the stones in the cemetery, here. Ivy-covered walls. The ball game on the radio, and I hate sports. You can't do like the women in TV movies who get wounded by a love affair and come back to the family home. My family home has been remodeled, just like Coe Hill. My elementary school is condos. My mother's in a "retirement community" so tasteful, so silent, it's like a funeral parlor. Don't you ever wish you'd left? Besides Pennsylvania, I mean. When you were young?

JO: Not in the end.

STEVEN: What did you do about loneliness?

JO: What *did* I do? I'll tell you what I *do* do. I do what I've always done. I have myself. I have friends. Work. I always loved to read. And church and the choir. Music. Music. I have a full day, every day.

STEVEN: I see. I do.

JO: Why don't I get my keys, and I can take you back over to Bloomfield in the truck?

STEVEN: No. Please. I prefer to walk.

JO: To *Bloomfield*?

STEVEN: It's not far. There's a science special on tonight. Stuff I have to know, to be good. You never had a TV, did you?

JO: Still don't. Get weather from the radio. Mostly I listen. Hemlocks in the wind. Geese. The Olsons' dog. A shutter in the sleet.

STEVEN: They don't have shutters where I live. It just comes down. And if a dog barks I resent it. No, I fear it. And I certainly don't know whose it is! [*Moves toward the door.*]

JO: Let me drive you.

STEVEN: Okay. Sure. Yes.

JO: Have to go out anyway.

STEVEN: Thank you. The night he left, he moved the last things, he said, "I hope you find what you need." I never loved him for anything like I loved him for leaving.

JO: I will not leave you comfortless. [*She exits.*]

STEVEN: Jo?

JO [*off*]: Just a minute.

STEVEN: I . . . I had other reasons. . .

JO [*off, but quite clearly*]: I know, Sport.

STEVEN: . . . for telling. For telling—

JO [*off*]: I know.

After a moment JO enters, in her late thirties again, as we saw her in The Snow Queen. *She has a large peanut-butter cookie in her hand.*

JO: Okay, now, Sport, there's one last thing we need to do to help the garden grow.

STEVEN [*with adult voice and bearing*]: What?

JO [*speaking to an unseen little boy*]: Sacrifice the Sacred Peanut-Butter Cookie to the Kale Gods!

STEVEN: Sacrifice?

JO: Oh, don't worry. Don't tell the Gods, but we keep it and eat it. Now: there is an ancient Siamese chant that goes with it, or it doesn't work. Want to hear it? Thought you'd never ask. It goes like this. [*Holds up the peanut-butter cookie.*] Oh-wah! Ta-goo! Siam! Come on, say it with me!

STEVEN and JO: Oh-wah! Ta-goo! Siam!

JO: Now faster . . .

They chant the phrase faster and faster until they are obviously chanting "Oh, what a goose I am." They laugh. JO breaks off a piece of cookie and holds it out to invisible little Steven.

JO: Have some, Sport.

STEVEN [*reaches, but can't quite get it*]: I was so jealous of her . . . and you.

JO: Yes.

STEVEN: You and I were the two people no one loved. I didn't think I ever could. And then, suddenly, someone loved you and you loved them. And in my family, when something is wrong, it is wrong. And I had to tell. No one tricked anyone. No one took advantage of me. I just had to.

JO: Of course you did. Of course you did.

STEVEN: And I am so, so sorry, Jo . . . [*Moves toward her.*] Even Moose. I can't be too sorry. I didn't know him, really. Because I was jealous of him.

JO: It's all right. [*She puts her arms around imaginary little Steven. Adult STEVEN kneels and slips into her encircling arms, and they hold each other.*]

STEVEN: Jealousy. [*Sighs. Shakes head.*] My God!

JO: The table of noes is a wondrous thing. You see, Sport?

STEVEN: Yes. Thank you.

BOTH [*singing; JO begins, STEVEN joins in*]:

> In the bleak midwinter, frosty wind made moan.
> Earth stood hard as iron, water like a stone.
> Snow had fallen, snow upon snow.
> In the bleak midwinter [*pause*] long ago.

Silence. They don't move.

Blackout.

End of play.

Acknowledgments

My thanks to the incomparable Jane Lincoln Taylor, who played Jo in the world premiere productions of both plays. Her commitment, her wisdom, and her artistry were an integral part of the experience for me and for our very appreciative audiences.

Thanks to Regie Cabico for selecting *The Snow Queen* for the 2003 "Writers on the Ledge" series produced by HERE Arts Center (Kristin Marting, founding artistic director) and Dixon Place (Ellie Covan, founder and artistic director). Thanks to the staffs and crews of both theaters for their work on the original productions.

Thanks to Neige Torrey Christenson for granting me permission to use the woodcut *John Roberts' Farm*, created by her mother, Margot Green Torrey.

Thanks to Nicholas Williams for making the cover look better than anything I could have imagined.

Thanks to Kelly Smith and Ann McMan for their usual spot-on work on, respectively, the inside and the outside of the book.

Thanks to Ellen McLaughlin for her great support.

Thanks as always to Rogério Pinto for his love and support and for the home he has made with me.

About the Author

David Pratt is the author of the novels *Todd Sweeney, the Fiend of Fleet High,* (Hosta Press) *Wallaçonia* (Beautiful Dreamer Press), *Looking After Joey* (Lethe Press) and the Lambda Literary Award-winning *Bob the Book* (Chelsea Station Editions). David's story collection, *My Movie* (Chelsea Station) includes new work and short fiction originally published in *Christopher Street, The James White Review, Velvet Mafia, Lodestar Quarterly* and other periodicals. Recent anthology publications include Louis Flint Ceci's *Not Just Another Pretty Face*, Jameson Currier's *With*, and *Short Story Book Project: Horror* from Breaking Rules Publishing.

David has directed and performed his work for the theater in New York City at the Cornelia Café, HERE Arts Center and Dixon Place, and in the NY International Fringe Festival, and he was the first director of plays by acclaimed Canadian playwright John Mighton. David recently performed with Michigan artist Nicholas Williams at The Forge in Detroit, Michigan.

WALLAÇONIA
a novel
DAVID PRATT

"The voyage of a boy who wins his own sense of manhood. A wonderfully written, original coming-of-age tale."
—*Lambda Literary Review*

"Sharp. Focused. Super-intense, and special. It's rare to find a novel with such a beautifully rendered friendship between a young gay man and an older mentor."
—Bill Konigsburg, author of *Openly Straight* and *The Porcupine of Truth*

Wallaçonia cover photo by Dot

Beautiful Dreamer Press

www.BeautifulDreamerPress.com